# MR. FERGUSSON HARDY

## A TALE THAT'S ABOUT FERGUSSON HARDY

SAMANTHA HARDY

tellwell

Tellwell Talent
www.tellwell.ca

ISBN
978-1-77302-550-6 (Paperback)
978-1-77302-551-3 (Hardcover)

DEDICATED TO:
SUSAN B. AND HER
    PRECIOUS CAT "PRECIOUS,"
CAROL T., DIANE S., PENNY M., STEPHEN K.,
BRUCE AND JUDY H., AND LEOPOLD B.

HONORARY MENTION TO:
DAEMON M., RAEANNE P., AMANDA R.,
    FRANCESCA J., LIVIU P.,
        NATASHA M., AND BOBBY B.

ILLUSTRATIONS
    AND NARRATIVE
        BY: SAMANTHA HARDY
DIGITAL FILES
    AND PHOTOGRAPHS
        BY: BRUCE HIPKIN

# HELLO

MY NAME IS SAMANTHA AND I HAVE A YOUNG CAT...

## HIS NAME IS..

# FERGUSSON

FOR SOME REASON I USUALLY CALL HIM...
MR. FERGUSSON

WHAT CAN I SAY ABOUT FERGUSSON?

## OH MY...

## HERE GOES...

HE IS 2 YEARS OLD

HE IS SUPER

FURRY

HE IS SO ADORABLE

WHAT I NOTICE THE MOST ABOUT HIS FACE... ARE... HIS EYES...

BECAUSE...

HIS FURRY FACE IS BLACK
HIS NOSE IS BLACK
HIS MOUTH IS BLACK
HIS WHISKERS ARE BLACK

EYES OPEN

EYES CLOSED

FRONT

BACK

FROM BEHIND...
TO ME IT SEEMS AS THOUGH
FERGUSSON IS WEARING
GREY FURRY PANTS

SO ADORABLE

AND IF I STAND AT THE ENTRANCE WHERE THE FAMILY ROOM ADJOINS THE KITCHEN AND I CALL...

"FERGUSSON"

THEN... SOMETIMES FERGUSSON HURRIES OVER TO MEET ME.

GOOD BOY

AND

SOMETIMES INTO HIS FOOD OR WATER DISH.... FERGUSSON WILL PUT...

ONE OF HIS TOYS

SOMETIMES FROM HIS FOOD DISH, FERGUSSON SOMETIMES TAKES A MOUTHFUL OF FOOD... AND THEN... HE DROPS IT ONTO THE FLOOR... AND THEN HE EATS IT!!!

SOMETIMES FERGUSSON MOVES HIS FOOD DISH AWAY FROM HIS WATER BOWL...

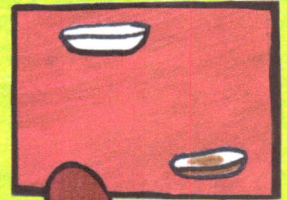

WOW

ONE TIME HE MOVED HIS FOOD DISH... TO THE MIDDLE OF THE KITCHEN FLOOR!

MR. FERGUSSON PREFERS TO HAVE HIS FOOD SLIGHTLY SOGGY...

SO I STIR A SMALL SPOONFUL OF COOL WATER INTO HIS FOOD

HONESTLY

# FERGUSSON PLAYS WITH HIS TOYS

## HIS FAVOURITE TOYS ARE...

RED TOY

GOLD TOY

BLUE TOY

PINK TOY

SILVER TOY

MOST OF THE TIME HE CHASES AFTER HIS TOYS ON THE KITCHEN FLOOR...

# HOWEVER

THE MOST AMAZING AND HONEST-TO-GOODNESS GAME THAT FERGUSSON PLAYS WITH HIS TOYS IS WHEN ...

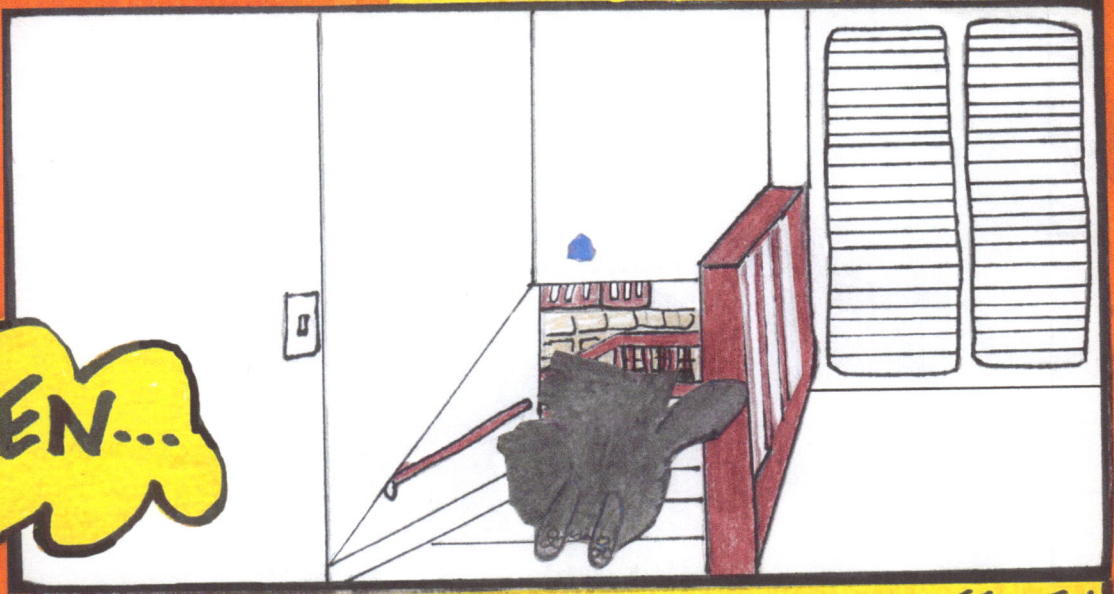

FERGUSSON TAKING IT EASY...

SO NOW YOU KNOW MR. FERGUSSON... HE REALLY IS A VERY SPECIAL
~~OWL~~
~~LION~~
~~CHICKEN~~
~~DOG~~
~~RACECAR~~
~~RAM~~
~~PERSON~~
CAT

FERGUSSON WAS BORN
IN JUNE 2015

CPSIA information can be obtained
at www.ICGtesting.com
Printed in the USA
LVHW05n1436050618
579580LV00005B/12/P

* 9 7 8 1 7 7 3 0 2 5 5 0 6 *